BUCHAREST TRAVEL GUIDE 2025

Experience the Best Attractions, Museums, Parks, Festivals, Dining, Day Trips and Outdoor Activities.

...ks, local secrets, vibrant nightlife, and practical tips for an immersive and unforgettable journey through Romania's captivating capital.

DANIEL BROWN

All rights reserved. No part of this book may be reproduced, stored in a retrieval system, or transmitted in any form or by any means, electronic, mechanical, photocopying, recording, or otherwise, without the prior written permission of the publisher, except for brief quotations in a book review.

Copyright © 2025 by DANIEL BROWN

TABLE OF CONTENTS

Welcome to Bucharest 6
Introduction to Bucharest 6
Why Visit in 2025? 7
A City Steeped in History and Culture 10

Getting to Bucharest 13
Flights and Airports 13
Train and Bus Travel 15
Visa and Entry Requirements 17

Navigating the City 20
Public Transportation 20
Car Rentals and Taxi Services 22
Walking Around 24

Top Attractions in Bucharest 27
Palace of the Parliament 27
Old Town (Lipscani) 29
Village Museum 31

Bucharest Travel Guide 2025

    Cismigiu Gardens and Herăstrău Park 34

    Stavropoleos Monastery 36

    Romanian Athenaeum 37

Cultural and Historical Insights 39

    The Rise and Fall of Communism 39

    Bucharest's Architecture 41

    Local Art and Museums 42

    Folklore and Traditions 44

Bucharest's Vibrant Nightlife 47

    Best Bars and Clubs in Old Town 47

    Live Music Venues 49

    Rooftop Bars and Cocktail Spots with Stunning Views 51

Local Cuisine and Dining Guide 54

    Must-Try Romanian Dishes 54

    Best Restaurants in Bucharest 57

    Street Food and Market Experiences 60

Vegetarian and Vegan Options in Bucharest . 62

Shopping in Bucharest 65

Souvenirs and Handmade Crafts..................... 65

High-End Boutiques and Local Designers 67

Best Shopping Malls and Markets for Every Budget... 69

Outdoor Activities and Day Trips............ 73

Walking and Biking Tours 73

Parks and Green Spaces for Relaxation 76

Day Trips from Bucharest 79

Accommodation 83

Luxury Hotels and Boutique Stays 83

Budget Hotels, Hostels, and Airbnbs 86

Neighborhood Guide....................................... 89

Seasonal Events and Festivals 92

Bucharest Music and Arts Festivals 93

Holiday Celebrations and Traditions 95

Best Times to Visit for Cultural Experiences . 98

Practical Travel Tips 101

Currency, ATMs, and Credit Cards................ 101

Safety Tips for Tourists 103

Health and Emergency Information 105

Internet, SIM Cards, and Staying Connected 107

Sample Itineraries 110

3 Days in Bucharest 110

5-Day Cultural and Historical Exploration ... 114

One Week in Bucharest.................................. 118

Weekend Getaways 121

Conclusion 124

Welcome to Bucharest

Introduction to Bucharest

Bucharest, Romania's dynamic capital, is a city of contrasts—a place where the old-world charm of centuries past sits side by side with the energy and innovation of modern life. This vibrant metropolis, once called the "Paris of the East," invites travelers to explore its tree-lined boulevards, grand architecture, and bustling streets. Whether it's your first time in Eastern Europe or you're a seasoned traveler, Bucharest will surprise you with its rich history, hidden gems, and lively atmosphere. From the majestic Palace of the Parliament to the cozy cafes in the Old Town, Bucharest is a city that promises to leave an impression on everyone who visits.

Known for its warm hospitality, Bucharest welcomes visitors with open arms. The locals, always ready to share a story or point you in the right direction, make the city feel personal and accessible, no matter how far you've come. Bucharest is more than a place on the map—it's a city with a pulse, where each neighborhood tells a story, every corner holds a secret, and every experience feels like a journey of discovery.

Whether you're wandering through its historic streets, tasting the local cuisine, or simply soaking in the unique atmosphere, you'll find that Bucharest is a city that grows on you. It's a destination that will surprise you in the best possible way, with its blend of history, culture, and modern vibrancy.

Why Visit in 2025?

2025 is shaping up to be an exciting year for Bucharest, making it the perfect time to explore Romania's capital. Post-pandemic recovery has brought a fresh wave of innovation, with new restaurants, cultural hubs, and events popping up all over the city. Tourism is booming, but Bucharest still offers a more authentic experience compared to its more tourist-saturated European counterparts. This gives visitors the unique opportunity to experience the city's charm without feeling overwhelmed by crowds.

In 2025, Bucharest will be hosting a variety of international events, music festivals, and art exhibitions that promise to elevate the city's already vibrant cultural scene. Whether you're a lover of the arts, history, or outdoor adventures, Bucharest has something for everyone. For foodies, the burgeoning culinary scene continues to evolve, with Romanian chefs blending traditional recipes with modern techniques, ensuring a unique gastronomic experience that's both delicious and memorable.

2025 also marks the opening of several new museums and galleries, offering deeper insights into Romania's history, from its ancient roots to its tumultuous 20th-century experiences. The city's parks and green spaces, always beloved by locals, are getting upgrades, making Bucharest an even more beautiful place to visit. Travelers can look forward to modern infrastructure improvements too, making it easier than ever to navigate the city and its surroundings.

Beyond the city's boundaries, Romania's natural beauty beckons, and Bucharest is the perfect gateway to the Carpathian Mountains, the serene Black Sea coast, and the enchanting castles of Transylvania. Whether you're planning a short trip or a longer journey, 2025 is a golden opportunity to discover Bucharest at its best—where tradition and progress blend seamlessly in a city that feels both exciting and familiar.

A City Steeped in History and Culture

Bucharest's history is as complex and layered as the city itself. Founded in the 15th century, it grew from a small settlement into a thriving city under the rule of Vlad the Impaler (yes, the inspiration behind Dracula). This period left a lasting imprint on Bucharest's character, with its early fortifications evolving into the city's modern-day defensive spirit. Over the centuries, Bucharest flourished as a center of culture, trade, and diplomacy, becoming Romania's capital in 1862.

Walking through Bucharest is like stepping back in time. The Old Town, with its narrow cobblestone streets and well-preserved medieval buildings, offers glimpses into Bucharest's past, while grand boulevards like Victory Avenue showcase its French-inspired architecture from the late 19th and early 20th centuries. It's easy to see why the city earned the nickname "Little Paris" during this period, as the elegant buildings, art nouveau designs, and broad streets evoke a Parisian feel.

Yet, Bucharest's history is not without its darker chapters. The city was profoundly shaped by the 20th century, particularly by the brutal communist regime of Nicolae Ceaușescu. His ambition to reshape Bucharest led to the construction of massive structures, most notably the Palace of the Parliament—an architectural feat and one of the largest buildings in the world. This era also saw the destruction of many historic areas, as entire neighborhoods were razed to make way for Ceaușescu's vision. While these scars are still visible, they also tell the story of resilience and rebirth. Today, Bucharest embraces its past while looking firmly toward the future, with post-communist revitalization breathing new life into the city.

Culturally, Bucharest is a melting pot where Romanian traditions meet modern influences. Festivals celebrating everything from jazz to traditional Romanian folk music are regular occurrences, and the city's theaters and concert halls are filled with events year-round. Museums, like the National Museum of Romanian History and the Village Museum, offer deep dives into Romania's heritage, while contemporary galleries showcase the works of modern Romanian artists who are making waves internationally.

This blend of history and culture is what makes Bucharest so captivating. Every monument, building, and street corner seems to have a story to tell—some tragic, others triumphant, but all fascinating. Whether you're delving into the communist era, exploring medieval landmarks, or enjoying a classical concert at the Romanian Athenaeum, you'll find that Bucharest is a city that wears its history proudly, yet continues to evolve.

Getting to Bucharest

Flights and Airports

How to Reach Bucharest

For most international travelers, arriving in Bucharest by air is the most convenient option. The city is served by **Henri Coandă International Airport (OTP)**, located about 18 kilometers (11 miles) north of the city center. As Romania's busiest and largest airport, Henri Coandă connects Bucharest to a wide range of international destinations across Europe, the Middle East, and even some parts of Asia and Africa. Whether you're flying from major hubs like London, Paris, or New York, or from smaller regional airports, you'll find direct flights or convenient connections to Bucharest.

Many major airlines operate frequent flights to and from Bucharest, including well-known carriers like British Airways, Lufthansa, and Turkish Airlines. For budget-conscious travelers, low-cost airlines like Wizz Air, Ryanair, and easyJet offer affordable fares, particularly if you're flying from within Europe. These budget airlines often have frequent deals, making Bucharest a surprisingly economical destination to reach, especially if you book early.

Once you arrive at Henri Coandă International, getting into the city is straightforward. The airport is well-connected to Bucharest's center via taxis, rideshares, and public transport. A quick and affordable option is the express bus, the **783** line, which runs regularly and takes you to key points in the city, such as **Piața Unirii**. For those seeking a more direct route, taxis and rideshare services like Uber are available right outside the arrivals area. The ride into central Bucharest typically takes around 30 to 40 minutes, depending on traffic, and costs about €15 to €20.

For those with connections through Europe, **Aurel Vlaicu International Airport (BBU)**, also known as **Băneasa Airport**, serves as an alternative for charter flights and private aviation, though it's much smaller and less frequently used for commercial travel.

Train and Bus Travel

Exploring Romania by Rail and Road

If you're traveling to Bucharest from neighboring countries or other parts of Romania, taking the train or bus can be a scenic and stress-free way to arrive. Romania's rail network, operated by **CFR (Căile Ferate Române)**, connects Bucharest with many European cities, including Budapest, Sofia, and Vienna. Trains to and from these major hubs run daily, and while journey times can be longer compared to flights, the comfort and experience of traveling by train offer a different perspective. For example, the train from Budapest to Bucharest takes about 15 hours, but the sweeping views of the Carpathian Mountains and rural Romania make it a picturesque journey.

Bucharest's main train station, **Gara de Nord**, is centrally located and well-connected to public transport, making it easy to transition from your train journey into city exploration. For those traveling domestically within Romania, Bucharest is a hub for both fast intercity trains (IR) and the slower, more affordable regional trains. If you're coming from cities like Brașov, Cluj-Napoca, or Constanța, the train is a comfortable and efficient way to get to the capital, and it offers the chance to enjoy Romania's scenic countryside.

Buses are another popular option, particularly for budget travelers. International bus lines like **Eurolines** and **FlixBus** provide connections between Bucharest and cities throughout Europe. Buses are generally cheaper than trains or flights, though travel times can be long, especially if you're coming from farther away. That said, buses tend to have frequent schedules and can be a convenient choice for those looking to save money on transport.

Within Romania, buses are often used for shorter trips or routes not well-served by trains. From cities like Brașov or Sibiu, buses to Bucharest are frequent, inexpensive, and take around 3 to 5 hours. Most long-distance buses arrive at **Autogara Filaret** or **Autogara Militari**, which are both relatively close to the city center and accessible by public transport.

Whether you're arriving by train or bus, you'll find that Bucharest's transit systems are easy to navigate and well-connected, ensuring a smooth journey into the heart of the city.

Visa and Entry Requirements

Before you embark on your Bucharest adventure, it's important to check the visa and entry requirements specific to your country of origin. Romania is a member of the **European Union**, though it is not part of the **Schengen Area**. This means that while Romania follows many EU guidelines, there are distinct rules when it comes to visas and border control.

For citizens of most European Union and European Economic Area (EEA) countries, as well as countries like the United States, Canada, and Australia, entry into Romania for tourism purposes is relatively straightforward. **No visa is required** for stays of up to 90 days within a 180-day period. This gives travelers ample time to explore Bucharest and even venture beyond the city to discover the wonders of Romania's countryside.

If you're traveling from a country that does require a visa, such as India or China, you'll need to apply for a **short-stay visa (C-type)** before your trip. The process involves providing documentation such as proof of accommodation, a return flight ticket, travel insurance, and evidence of sufficient financial means for the duration of your stay. Visa processing times can vary, so it's recommended to apply at least a few weeks before your intended travel date to ensure you have everything in place.

Romania has a number of **visa exemptions** and agreements in place, so it's always worth checking the latest updates from the **Romanian Ministry of Foreign Affairs** or consulting with your local Romanian embassy or consulate. Keep in mind that even if you don't require a visa, border control officers may ask for proof of onward travel or sufficient funds for your stay, so it's a good idea to have these documents easily accessible.

Once you've cleared immigration and are in Romania, the country offers relatively hassle-free travel for tourists. If you plan on exploring other parts of Europe after your time in Bucharest, it's important to note that Romania operates under its own border policies, meaning you'll need to show your passport or ID when crossing into Schengen countries.

Whether you're arriving by plane, train, or bus, getting to Bucharest is the start of an exciting journey, and with the right preparation, you'll find the process smooth and straightforward.

Navigating the City

Public Transportation

Metro, Buses, and Trams

Bucharest's public transportation system is a fantastic way to explore the city, offering both convenience and affordability. The city's network includes **metros, buses, trams, and trolleybuses**, all of which are well integrated and widely used by locals and tourists alike. Whether you're heading to a historical site, a cozy cafe, or one of the city's sprawling parks, Bucharest's public transportation makes it easy to get around.

The **Metro** is perhaps the most efficient and straightforward way to travel, especially for visitors. Operated by **Metrorex**, Bucharest's metro system is clean, reliable, and covers the major areas of the city. There are **five metro**

lines (M1, M2, M3, M4, and M5), and they operate from early morning until around 11:00 PM. The M2 line is particularly useful for tourists, as it runs through key areas like **Piața Unirii**, **Piața Victoriei**, and **Universitate**, all of which are close to many of Bucharest's major attractions.

Fares are inexpensive and easy to manage. You can purchase single tickets, day passes, or even a **10-trip card** depending on the length of your stay. One of the conveniences of the metro is the availability of automated ticket machines and even contactless payments with a card, making it quick and hassle-free to get where you need to go.

The **bus and tram system** is extensive, with over **100 bus lines** and **20 tram lines** serving different parts of the city. Operated by **STB (Societatea de Transport București)**, buses and trams are a great option if you're traveling to areas not covered by the metro or if you want to experience the city above ground. Buses, trams, and trolleybuses are usually quite frequent, although traffic in Bucharest can slow down some routes during rush hour.

To use buses and trams, you'll need an **STB travel card**, which can be reloaded as needed and is valid on all STB transport. You can purchase these cards at kiosks located near major stops or at metro stations. Remember to validate your card as you board to avoid fines.

One of the joys of using public transportation in Bucharest is that it lets you blend in with the locals, seeing the city from their perspective. It's not uncommon to strike up a conversation with a fellow passenger or get a recommendation for a great restaurant or hidden attraction. Plus, riding a tram along Bucharest's historic routes can offer unexpected glimpses of the city's architecture and daily life that you'd miss otherwise.

Car Rentals and Taxi Services
What You Need to Know

While public transport is a great option, sometimes you'll want the flexibility of a car, especially if you plan on taking day trips outside of Bucharest. **Car rentals** are widely available in the city, and most major international car rental companies like **Avis**, **Hertz**, and **Sixt** have offices at **Henri Coandă International Airport** and in central Bucharest. Renting a car can be an excellent way to explore Romania's scenic countryside, with easy access to places like **Snagov**, **Mogosoaia Palace**, or even further afield to **Transylvania**.

However, driving in Bucharest comes with its challenges. Traffic can be heavy, particularly during rush hours, and the city's road system can be a bit chaotic, especially for those not used to it. Parking can also be tricky in the city center, with limited spaces and many streets requiring a paid parking permit. It's worth checking with your hotel or accommodation to see if they offer parking or have recommendations for nearby garages.

If you do decide to drive, make sure you're familiar with Romanian driving laws. Speed limits in urban areas are typically 50 km/h (about 31 mph), and there are strict **zero-tolerance** policies for drinking and driving. Road signs are fairly standard, and GPS services like **Google Maps** work well across the city and country.

If renting a car sounds like too much hassle, **taxis** and **rideshares** are abundant and affordable. Bucharest's taxis are easy to spot—yellow cars with company logos and fares printed on the side. Make sure to choose a taxi from a reputable company like

Speed Taxi, **Meridian**, or **Cristaxi**, and always check that the meter is running. Taxis can be hailed from the street, found at taxi ranks, or called using a phone app.

For added convenience, many visitors prefer using rideshare services like **Uber**, **Bolt**, or **Free Now**. These apps are widely used in Bucharest and can help you avoid misunderstandings with language or payment. The rates are reasonable, and the added benefit of tracking your trip and knowing the fare upfront makes it a stress-free way to get around the city, especially late at night or when you have luggage.

While car rentals and taxis provide flexibility, Bucharest's public transportation and walkability often make them unnecessary unless you're heading out of town.

Walking Around
The Best Way to Experience Bucharest

Though Bucharest has a robust transportation network, there's something magical about exploring the city on foot. In fact, walking is often the best way to experience the heart of Bucharest, especially in **Old Town (Lipscani)**, where narrow streets, hidden alleyways, and charming historical buildings create an atmosphere that's perfect for wandering. This pedestrian-friendly zone is a maze of boutiques, cafes, and restaurants, each offering its own slice of Bucharest's vibrant life. You can easily spend hours here, discovering something new around every corner, from quaint bookshops to centuries-old churches.

Strolling along the grand **Victory Avenue (Calea Victoriei)** offers a different kind of experience, one that takes you past some of the city's most important landmarks, including the **National Museum of Romanian History**, the **Romanian Athenaeum**, and the **Cercul Militar Național**. This is a great way to admire the city's mix of architectural styles, from neoclassical grandeur to communist-era monuments.

Bucharest's many **parks and gardens** also make walking a delight. **Herăstrău Park** (recently renamed King Michael I Park), located near the **Village Museum**, offers long paths that wind around a large lake, perfect for leisurely walks or picnics. In the heart of the city, **Cismigiu Gardens** is a favorite spot for locals and tourists alike, with its picturesque pathways, peaceful lake, and old-world charm. It's a wonderful place to take a break from the bustling city streets, enjoy a coffee, or people-watch.

The best part about walking in Bucharest is that it allows you to see the city in a way that no other form of transportation can. You can take in the small details—the smell of freshly baked **covrigi** (Romanian pretzels) from street vendors, the sound of church bells echoing through narrow streets, or the sight of lively outdoor cafes buzzing with conversation. Walking gives you the freedom to stop whenever something catches your eye, whether it's a vibrant mural on a side street or a cozy bar offering the perfect spot to relax.

Overall, while Bucharest offers plenty of transportation options, there's no better way to experience the city's soul than on foot. It's here, in the small moments of discovery, that you'll truly feel connected to this vibrant and ever-evolving city.

Top Attractions in Bucharest

Palace of the Parliament

A Monument of Political Power

Standing as both a symbol of Romania's communist past and a stunning architectural feat, the **Palace of the Parliament** is a must-see for anyone visiting Bucharest. Built under the regime of **Nicolae Ceaușescu**, this colossal structure is the **second-largest administrative building in the world**, surpassed only by the Pentagon. Covering a staggering 365,000 square meters (about 4 million square feet), the Palace dominates the city's skyline, embodying both grandeur and controversy.

The building is not just massive; it's intricately designed. The interiors feature over **3,000 rooms**, and many of them boast extravagant decorations such as marble floors, crystal chandeliers, and gold-plated elements. Guided tours take visitors through the grand halls and chambers, offering a glimpse into the excesses of Ceaușescu's regime. One of the highlights is the **Union Hall**, a vast space with towering ceilings that was intended to host grand political gatherings.

While the Palace of the Parliament is an architectural marvel, its history adds another layer of fascination. Constructed during the 1980s, it was built at the expense of ordinary Romanians, many of whom suffered due to the massive costs associated with its construction. Thousands of homes, churches, and historical buildings were destroyed to make room for Ceaușescu's vision, and many Romanians still feel conflicted about the legacy it left behind.

Despite its controversial past, the Palace has become one of Bucharest's most iconic landmarks. It currently houses **Romania's Parliament** as well as the **National Museum of Contemporary Art (MNAC)**. When visiting, be sure to take in the panoramic view of **Bulevardul Unirii** from the balcony, a perfect spot for appreciating the scale of both the building and the urban landscape Ceaușescu reshaped.

Old Town (Lipscani)

A Walk Through Bucharest's History

Wandering through **Old Town (Lipscani)** is like stepping back in time. This vibrant and historical area of Bucharest offers a fascinating glimpse into the city's past, while also serving as a lively hub for restaurants, bars, and boutique shops. Named after the merchants who once sold their goods here, Lipscani is a delightful mix of **medieval streets, 19th-century architecture**, and modern-day energy.

As you stroll through the narrow, cobblestone streets, you'll encounter a wide variety of historical buildings, from centuries-old inns to grand merchant houses. The contrast between Bucharest's Ottoman influences and its neoclassical designs becomes evident in Lipscani, where former banks, theaters, and old warehouses are now transformed into trendy spots for dining and shopping.

A visit to Old Town isn't complete without stopping by the **Manuc's Inn (Hanul lui Manuc)**, one of the oldest inns in Bucharest, which has been serving travelers since the early 19th century. Today, it's a beautiful reminder of the city's longstanding tradition of hospitality, with its charming courtyard and atmospheric architecture.

As day turns into night, Lipscani comes alive with a vibrant nightlife scene. Bars, cafes, and live music venues line the streets, making it a perfect spot for visitors to experience both the historic charm and the modern pulse of Bucharest. Whether you're here to soak up the city's history or simply to enjoy a coffee in a quaint café, Old Town offers a truly immersive experience.

Village Museum

Exploring Romania's Rural Heritage

For a peaceful escape from the bustling streets of the capital, the **Dimitrie Gusti National Village Museum** offers a unique opportunity to explore Romania's rural heritage. Located in the beautiful **Herăstrău Park**, this open-air museum is home to over **300 traditional houses**, barns, churches, and windmills, each carefully transported from various regions of Romania to preserve the country's rich cultural history.

Walking through the museum feels like stepping into a different era. The traditional wooden homes, some with thatched roofs and colorful exteriors, reflect the distinct architectural styles of Romania's diverse regions, from **Maramureş** in the north to **Dobrogea** on the Black Sea coast. As you explore the museum's expansive grounds, you'll gain insight into how rural Romanians lived centuries ago, with a focus on the country's unique folk traditions and craftsmanship.

One of the most interesting aspects of the Village Museum is the attention to detail. Inside some of the homes, you'll find original furnishings, pottery, and textiles that were used by Romanian villagers in their everyday lives. The museum also hosts **craft fairs**, traditional **folk music** performances, and special events throughout the year, offering a deeper connection to Romania's rural culture. Whether you're an architecture enthusiast or just looking to enjoy a peaceful afternoon surrounded by greenery, the Village Museum is a must-visit.

Cismigiu Gardens and Herăstrău Park
Bucharest's Green Retreats

Though Bucharest is a bustling metropolis, it also offers some tranquil green spaces where you can take a breather from the city's energy. **Cismigiu Gardens**, located in the heart of Bucharest, is a lush park with winding paths, serene lakes, and plenty of spots to relax. Dating back to the 19th century, Cismigiu is the city's oldest park and has a timeless charm. On any given day, you'll see locals enjoying a stroll, rowing boats on the lake, or simply unwinding with a good book under the shade of the trees.

The park is particularly beautiful in the spring and summer when the flowerbeds are in full bloom, adding bursts of color to the green landscape. For those looking to experience local life, the park's many benches offer a perfect vantage point to people-watch and absorb the slower rhythm of Bucharest outside of its busy streets.

Further north, **Herăstrău Park** (now officially known as **King Michael I Park**) offers a much larger green space that includes **Herăstrău Lake**. This is a favorite spot for both locals and tourists alike, especially during the warmer months when boating and outdoor activities are in full swing. Whether you're renting a paddleboat, enjoying a bike ride, or simply walking along the tree-lined paths, Herăstrău is the perfect place to escape the urban hustle and recharge in nature.

In addition to its beautiful natural scenery, Herăstrău Park is also home to the **Village Museum**, making it a great destination for a full day of exploration and relaxation. The park's many cafes, restaurants, and even an amusement park make it a popular spot for families and anyone looking to enjoy a leisurely afternoon.

Stavropoleos Monastery
A Hidden Gem of Spirituality

Tucked away in the bustling streets of Old Town, the **Stavropoleos Monastery** is one of Bucharest's most serene and beautiful spots. This small but exquisite Orthodox monastery was built in the early 18th century, and it's a prime example of **Brâncovenesc architecture**, which combines traditional Romanian and Byzantine styles with elements of the Ottoman era. The result is a stunning blend of intricate stonework, wooden carvings, and beautifully painted frescoes.

Although small in size, the monastery's courtyard offers a peaceful escape from the lively streets of Old Town. Surrounded by arches and vines, the courtyard feels almost otherworldly, a quiet sanctuary in the heart of the city. The church itself is equally mesmerizing, with its ornate icons, delicate frescoes, and hand-carved wooden details that showcase the artistry of the time.

Stavropoleos Monastery isn't just a place of worship—it's also a testament to Bucharest's rich religious history and the resilience of its spiritual heritage. Despite the challenges faced by the city over the centuries, this gem has stood the test of time, offering visitors a glimpse into a quieter, more contemplative side of Bucharest. Whether you're interested in architecture, history, or simply seeking a moment of peace, a visit to Stavropoleos is sure to leave a lasting impression.

Romanian Athenaeum

A Grand Concert Hall with a Rich Legacy

If you're a lover of classical music or simply appreciate grand architecture, the **Romanian Athenaeum** is a must-see. This iconic building is not only the heart of Romania's musical life but also one of Bucharest's most stunning architectural treasures. Built in the late 19th century, the Athenaeum is a neoclassical masterpiece, complete with grand columns, a beautifully domed roof, and intricate frescoes depicting key moments in Romanian history.

Inside, the concert hall is breathtaking. Its circular layout, adorned with golden accents and plush red velvet seats, creates an atmosphere of old-world elegance. The **Great Hall** can seat over 800 people and is renowned for its exceptional acoustics. Attending a concert here—whether it's a performance by the **George Enescu Philharmonic Orchestra** or one of the many international artists who perform throughout the year—is a truly unforgettable experience.

Beyond its role as a concert venue, the Romanian Athenaeum holds a deep connection to the cultural identity of Romania. It was built during a time when Romania was establishing itself as an independent nation, and it quickly became a symbol of the country's cultural aspirations. To this day, it remains a place where Romanians gather to celebrate the arts, and where visitors can feel the pulse of Bucharest's artistic soul.

Whether you attend a concert or simply tour the building, the Romanian Athenaeum offers a majestic journey into Bucharest's cultural heart.

Cultural and Historical Insights

The Rise and Fall of Communism

To truly understand Bucharest, one must first explore its complex and turbulent past, particularly the **era of communism** that shaped much of Romania's 20th-century history. The seeds of communism in Romania were sown in the aftermath of World War II when Soviet influence began to take hold in Eastern Europe. In 1947, **King Michael I** was forced to abdicate, and Romania was declared a socialist republic. What followed was decades of strict communist rule under leaders like **Gheorghe Gheorghiu-Dej** and later, **Nicolae Ceaușescu**.

The **Ceaușescu regime**, which began in 1965, is infamous for its repressive policies and harsh economic measures that deeply affected everyday life in Romania. Ceaușescu pursued an ambitious vision for modernization, symbolized by grandiose projects like the **Palace of the Parliament**, but his government was marked by widespread poverty, food shortages, and a brutal secret police known as the **Securitate**. Ordinary Romanians faced censorship, surveillance, and a lack of basic freedoms.

However, the regime's grip began to weaken by the late 1980s, when growing unrest across the country led to the **Romanian Revolution** in 1989. Massive protests broke out, and after a week of violent clashes, Ceaușescu and his wife, Elena, were captured, tried, and executed. This marked the end of communism in Romania and the beginning of a new era. Today, remnants of this period can still be felt throughout Bucharest—from the imposing architecture to the stories told by older generations. Museums like the **Memorial of the Victims of Communism** provide a poignant reminder of this dark chapter in Romania's history.

Bucharest's Architecture
From Neoclassical to Brutalist

Bucharest's architectural landscape tells the story of a city that has constantly evolved, with each era leaving its mark. Walking through the streets of Bucharest, you'll notice a fascinating mix of styles—from elegant **neoclassical buildings** that reflect Romania's royal past to the stark **brutalist architecture** that arose during the communist period.

In the late 19th and early 20th centuries, Bucharest was often referred to as **"Little Paris"** because of its many French-inspired buildings. The **Romanian Athenaeum**, **Cantacuzino Palace**, and the **CEC Palace** are some of the finest examples of **neoclassical and Beaux-Arts architecture** that characterized this golden age. These structures evoke a time when Romania was embracing European trends and solidifying its identity as an emerging nation.

However, this elegance is juxtaposed with the **concrete blocks and utilitarian designs** that dominate parts of Bucharest, a reminder of the city's communist era. Under Ceaușescu's rule, entire neighborhoods were demolished to make way for enormous housing complexes and government buildings. The **House of the Free Press** and the **Palace of the Parliament** stand as iconic examples of **brutalist architecture**, designed to showcase power and control rather than aesthetic beauty. While not as visually appealing as the older buildings, these structures are important symbols of Bucharest's history and the political forces that shaped it.

Despite the contrast, Bucharest's architecture is gradually undergoing restoration. Many historical buildings are being revitalized, while new, modern structures are being constructed. This blend of old and new creates a cityscape that is as dynamic as the culture itself—one that offers a unique visual journey through Romania's rich and tumultuous past.

Local Art and Museums

National Museum of Art, Museum of Romanian History, and More

For art enthusiasts and history buffs, Bucharest offers a wealth of museums that celebrate Romania's artistic and cultural heritage. At the forefront is the **National Museum of Art of Romania**, housed in the former **Royal Palace**. Here, you'll find an impressive collection of Romanian and European art, spanning centuries. From **medieval religious icons** to works by renowned Romanian painters like **Nicolae Grigorescu** and **Theodor Aman**, the museum provides a deep dive into Romania's artistic legacy. The **European Art Gallery** within the museum features masterpieces from artists like **El Greco**, **Rembrandt**, and **Rubens**, offering visitors a broader perspective on European art movements.

History lovers should not miss the **National Museum of Romanian History**. Located in a beautiful neoclassical building, the museum showcases over **60,000 years of Romanian history**, including archaeological treasures like the **Pietroasele Treasure**, a collection of gold artifacts from the 4th century. The museum also offers an in-depth look at Romania's modern history, including the rise of the nation-state in the 19th century and the communist era that followed. It's a captivating way to understand Romania's complex historical trajectory.

In addition to these major museums, Bucharest is home to smaller gems like the **Museum of the**

Romanian Peasant, which celebrates traditional rural life, and the **Zambaccian Museum**, which displays an eclectic collection of Romanian and international modern art. The city's vibrant arts scene continues to thrive, with contemporary galleries popping up across Bucharest, further enriching its cultural landscape.

Folklore and Traditions

Celebrating Romania's Heritage

Romania's folklore and traditions are an essential part of its national identity, and nowhere is this more evident than in Bucharest. Though a modern and cosmopolitan city, Bucharest still holds tight to the country's rich cultural roots, offering visitors a chance to experience Romanian customs and celebrations.

One of the most enchanting aspects of Romania's heritage is its folklore, which is deeply intertwined with rural life and nature. From **fairy tales** featuring mythical creatures like **dragons and fairies** to **seasonal festivals** that have been passed down through generations, Romanian folklore reflects a deep connection to the land and its people. Many of these traditions are celebrated during holidays like **Mărțișor** (March 1st), when Romanians exchange small red and white trinkets to welcome the arrival of spring, or **Dragobete** (February 24th), a Romanian version of Valentine's Day that honors love and fertility.

Music and dance also play a significant role in Romanian culture. Traditional folk music, featuring instruments like the **cobza** (a type of lute) and the **pan flute**, is often performed during festivals and village celebrations. **Hora**, a lively circle dance, is one of the most popular traditional dances, symbolizing unity and community.

For those looking to immerse themselves in Romania's cultural heritage, visiting during festivals like the **George Enescu Festival**—a prestigious classical music event—or the **National Day of Romania** on December 1st is a great way to experience the vibrancy of Romanian traditions. Throughout the city, you'll also find restaurants and markets that celebrate Romania's culinary heritage, from **sarmale** (stuffed cabbage rolls) to **mici** (grilled minced meat rolls).

Bucharest offers a window into Romania's soul, where the past and present blend seamlessly. The city's deep appreciation for its folklore and traditions is a reminder that, despite its rapid modernization, Romania remains a country proud of its cultural roots.

Bucharest's Vibrant Nightlife

Best Bars and Clubs in Old Town

Bucharest's **Old Town (Lipscani District)** is the heartbeat of the city's nightlife. Once the bustling commercial center of the city during the 15th and 16th centuries, today, its narrow, cobblestone streets are home to some of the most vibrant bars, pubs, and clubs in Bucharest. Whether you're looking for a casual drink in a cozy bar or a night filled with dancing, Old Town has something for every type of night owl.

One of the most famous spots in this area is **Nomad Skybar**, known for its chic, rooftop setting and lively atmosphere. Whether you're there for its signature cocktails or the live DJ sets, Nomad offers a trendy vibe that makes it a must-visit. For something more laid-back but equally entertaining, **Shoteria** is a great place to kick off your night. Specializing in a wide variety of shots, Shoteria brings a fun, energetic atmosphere that gets you in the party mood.

For a more classic, local experience, head to **Caru' cu Bere**, one of Bucharest's oldest beer halls. Nestled in a stunning Gothic Revival building, this bar is a favorite among locals and visitors alike. With its rich woodwork, stained-glass windows, and impressive beer selection, you can easily spend hours soaking up the history while enjoying a cold drink.

If dancing is more your speed, Bucharest's Old Town has a plethora of clubs where the party stretches into the early hours of the morning. **Beluga Music & Cocktails** is one of the hotspots for club-goers, offering a mix of electronic, house, and pop music that keeps the energy high. For a more underground feel, **Control Club** just outside Old Town provides a different experience, featuring alternative and indie music, often accompanied by live performances. With its raw, industrial vibe and diverse crowd, it's a haven for music lovers looking for a break from mainstream beats.

Live Music Venues

Jazz, Rock, and Traditional Sounds

Bucharest's nightlife isn't just about bars and clubs—it also boasts an incredible live music scene that caters to all tastes. Whether you're into smooth jazz, head-banging rock, or traditional Romanian folk music, the city offers a diverse array of live venues where talented musicians take the stage.

For jazz lovers, **Green Hours Jazz Café** is the ultimate destination. Tucked away on Calea Victoriei, this intimate venue has been a pillar of Bucharest's live music scene for years. Its cozy, dimly lit atmosphere makes it the perfect place to relax with a glass of wine and listen to soulful jazz performances by local and international artists. The café hosts regular concerts, showcasing everything from classic jazz to more experimental sounds.

If rock is more your style, **Quantic Club** is the go-to venue. Located a little outside the city center, Quantic is known for hosting rock and metal concerts, bringing together both local and international bands. The venue also has an outdoor area, making it an ideal spot for open-air festivals and summer concerts. It's a place where the Bucharest rock scene comes alive, offering something raw and authentic for those who crave high-energy performances.

Traditional Romanian music also has its place in Bucharest's nightlife. At **Taverna Covaci**, located in Old Town, you can experience live Romanian folk music while enjoying a traditional meal. From the sounds of the **cimbalom** (a traditional string instrument) to upbeat folk dances, this venue offers an immersive cultural experience. It's a great way to dive into Romania's rich musical traditions while savoring the country's authentic flavors.

If you're looking for a more eclectic mix, **The Expirat Club** combines live music with a dynamic nightlife scene. Offering both live band performances and DJ sets, Expirat bridges the gap between concert venue and nightclub. You'll find a range of genres here, from indie rock to electronic, all within a lively and welcoming atmosphere.

Rooftop Bars and Cocktail Spots with Stunning Views

When it comes to experiencing Bucharest's nightlife in style, nothing beats sipping cocktails at a rooftop bar while taking in the stunning city views. Bucharest's growing rooftop scene has made it a favorite destination for those looking for a more refined nightlife experience, combining beautiful scenery with craft cocktails and chic settings.

One of the most popular rooftop spots in Bucharest is the **Linea / Closer to the Moon**, which offers breathtaking panoramic views of the city's skyline. Located atop the **Victoria Department Store**, this stylish bar is a perfect place to unwind with a drink while watching the sun set over the city. Whether you're sipping on a signature cocktail like their famous **Midnight in Bucharest** or enjoying a glass of Romanian wine, Linea is an ideal spot for a relaxed yet elegant night out.

Another must-visit rooftop bar is **Pura Vida Sky Bar**, located in the heart of Old Town. This laid-back venue offers a more casual vibe but doesn't skimp on the views. The bohemian décor, combined with a wide selection of drinks, makes it a great spot to hang out with friends and enjoy the cool evening breeze. As you sip your cocktail, you'll be treated to stunning views of the historic buildings that make up Bucharest's Old Town.

For a sophisticated night out, head to **E3 by Entourage**, a rooftop bar offering both elegance and exclusivity. With its sleek, modern design and curated cocktail menu, E3 caters to a chic crowd looking for a high-end experience. The terrace offers unobstructed views of **Herastrau Park** and the northern part of the city, making it a favorite among locals and expats alike.

If you're in the mood for something a bit more creative, **DESCHIS Gastrobar** offers a unique mix of food, drinks, and art. Situated on top of an old industrial building, this rooftop bar blends a casual atmosphere with innovative cocktails and a menu full of local and international flavors. DESCHIS is not just about the drinks; it's a cultural hub where art installations, film screenings, and live performances take place regularly.

These rooftop bars provide a different perspective on Bucharest's nightlife, offering an escape from the energetic streets below. They allow you to take in the beauty of the city in a more relaxed and refined environment, where every sip is accompanied by an unforgettable view.

Local Cuisine and Dining Guide

Must-Try Romanian Dishes
From Sarmale to Mici

No visit to Bucharest is complete without indulging in the delightful and hearty Romanian cuisine. Romanian food is a hearty blend of Eastern European and Mediterranean flavors, with dishes that are both comforting and full of character. Here are some quintessential Romanian dishes you simply must try:

1. Sarmale

Imagine a dish that combines tender cabbage leaves with a savory filling of minced pork, rice, and a mix of spices, all simmered slowly in a tangy tomato sauce. That's sarmale, one of Romania's most beloved dishes. Each bite of sarmale reveals layers of flavor that have been developed through hours of cooking. Often served with a dollop of sour cream and a side of polenta (mămăligă), sarmale is the epitome of Romanian comfort food.

2. Mici

Known as Romanian grilled sausages, mici (pronounced "meech") are a must-try. These sausages are made from a mix of beef, pork, and sometimes lamb, seasoned with garlic, thyme, and other spices. Grilled to perfection, they're often enjoyed with mustard and fresh bread. Mici are perfect for a casual meal and are commonly found at street food stalls, bars, and during summer barbecues.

3. Ciorbă de Burtă

If you're feeling adventurous, try ciorbă de burtă, a traditional Romanian tripe soup. This rich and creamy soup is made with beef tripe, vegetables, and is flavored with vinegar, garlic, and a touch of sour cream. It's an acquired taste, but for many Romanians, it's a beloved dish that brings comfort and nostalgia.

4. Cozonaci

For dessert, don't miss cozonaci, a sweet, yeast-leavened bread filled with a rich mixture of walnuts, cocoa, and sometimes raisins. Typically enjoyed during holidays like Christmas and Easter, cozonaci is a treat that's both festive and comforting.

Romanian cuisine is a celebration of flavors and traditions, offering dishes that are deeply rooted in the country's history and culture.

Best Restaurants in Bucharest

Fine Dining to Hidden Gems

Bucharest's dining scene is a rich tapestry that caters to all tastes and budgets. Whether you're in the mood for an elegant fine dining experience or a cozy meal at a hidden gem, the city's restaurants offer a diverse array of options.

1. Fine Dining

The Artist

For a high-end dining experience, The Artist offers a contemporary twist on Romanian cuisine. With a focus on innovative dishes and presentation, this Michelin-recognized restaurant provides an elegant setting where each meal is a work of art. From the amuse-bouche to the carefully crafted main courses, The Artist promises a memorable culinary journey.

Savoy

Another top choice for fine dining is Savoy, known for its classic French-inspired menu and luxurious ambiance. Located in a beautifully restored building, Savoy offers an exquisite dining experience with dishes prepared using the finest ingredients. The wine list is equally impressive, featuring a selection of international and Romanian wines.

2. Hidden Gems

Hanu' lui Manuc

A true gem tucked away in the Old Town, Hanu' lui Manuc combines historical charm with delicious traditional Romanian dishes. This historic inn, dating back to 1808, offers a unique atmosphere and a menu that features hearty Romanian classics. The restaurant's traditional décor and warm hospitality make it a fantastic spot to enjoy dishes like sarmale and mici.

Lacrimi și Sfinți

For a more casual yet equally delightful experience, Lacrimi și Sfinți (Tears and Saints) offers a cozy ambiance with a menu that highlights the flavors of Romanian comfort food. The restaurant's dishes are crafted with a modern twist, and the warm, rustic setting adds to the overall charm.

Shift Pub

If you're looking for a laid-back atmosphere with great food and drinks, Shift Pub is a popular spot among locals. Known for its creative dishes and relaxed vibe, Shift Pub is perfect for a casual meal or a night out with friends. The menu features a mix of Romanian and international dishes, and the cocktails are a standout.

Street Food and Market Experiences
Where to Find Authentic Flavors

For an authentic taste of Bucharest, exploring the street food scene and local markets is a must. These vibrant spots offer a glimpse into everyday Romanian life and the chance to sample a variety of delicious and affordable dishes.

1. Street Food

Obor Market

One of Bucharest's largest and most traditional markets, Obor Market is a bustling hub where you can find a variety of street food and local specialties. From freshly made mici and traditional sausages to sweet treats like papanasi (fried doughnuts with cheese and jam), Obor Market is a food lover's paradise. The market's lively atmosphere adds to the experience, making it a great place to immerse yourself in local flavors.

Piața Amzei

Another great spot for street food is Piața Amzei, a market that offers a range of local and international foods. It's a wonderful place to sample fresh produce, cheeses, and cured meats.

Many food stalls also offer traditional Romanian snacks and pastries, making it a great stop for a quick and tasty bite.

2. Market Experiences

Mănăstirea Caşin Market

For a more intimate market experience, Mănăstirea Caşin Market offers a selection of artisanal products and local delicacies. This market focuses on high-quality, often organic products, including cheeses, cured meats, and baked goods. It's a perfect place to pick up unique ingredients or enjoy a leisurely meal.

Bucharest Farmers' Market

Held at various locations throughout the city, the Bucharest Farmers' Market showcases local produce and artisanal foods. It's a great place to sample fresh fruits and vegetables, homemade cheeses, and baked goods. The market also features a range of traditional Romanian dishes, providing an opportunity to taste the country's culinary diversity.

Vegetarian and Vegan Options in Bucharest

Bucharest is increasingly becoming more inclusive for vegetarians and vegans, with a growing number of restaurants and cafés offering plant-based options. Here are some top spots where you can enjoy delicious and innovative vegetarian and vegan dishes:

1. Vegetarian Restaurants

Simbio

A stylish and popular spot, Simbio offers a variety of vegetarian and vegan dishes in a chic setting. The menu features creative options like vegan burgers, fresh salads, and flavorful bowls. The café's relaxed atmosphere makes it a great place for a leisurely lunch or dinner.

Lacrimi și Sfinți

In addition to its traditional Romanian fare, Lacrimi și Sfinți also offers a range of vegetarian options. The restaurant's menu includes dishes like stuffed peppers and vegetarian ciorbă (sour soup), showcasing the versatility of Romanian cuisine.

2. Vegan-Friendly Cafés

Rawdia

Rawdia specializes in raw and vegan cuisine, offering a range of dishes made from fresh, organic ingredients. From vibrant salads and wraps to decadent raw desserts, Rawdia caters to those looking for healthy and cruelty-free options.

Bio Fresh

Another excellent choice for vegan and vegetarian dining is Bio Fresh, which focuses on organic and plant-based dishes. The café offers a variety of smoothies, salads, and vegan main courses, all made from high-quality, organic ingredients.

Bucharest's culinary scene is rich and diverse, offering something for everyone, whether you're a foodie looking to explore traditional Romanian flavors or someone seeking vegetarian and vegan options. The city's dining experiences range from elegant fine dining to vibrant street food, ensuring that every meal is an adventure in itself.

Shopping in Bucharest

Bucharest is a city where shopping goes beyond just filling your suitcase. It's about finding unique treasures, indulging in luxury, and experiencing the vibrant local culture through its markets and boutiques. Whether you're hunting for souvenirs, exploring high-end fashion, or navigating bustling shopping malls, Bucharest offers something for every shopper.

Souvenirs and Handmade Crafts

When it comes to souvenirs, Bucharest has a rich array of options that capture the essence of Romanian culture and craftsmanship. Here's a guide to some of the best items to consider bringing home:

1. Traditional Romanian Crafts

- **Handmade Pottery**: Romanian pottery, especially from the regions of Horezu and Corund, is known for its intricate designs and vibrant colors. These pieces often feature traditional motifs and are perfect for adding a touch of Romanian artistry to your home. Look for handcrafted pots, bowls, and vases that showcase the local craftsmanship.

- **Embroidery and Textiles**: Romanian embroidery is a reflection of the country's folk traditions. You can find beautifully embroidered tablecloths, pillowcases, and garments, often adorned with geometric patterns and bright colors. These textiles make for unique and meaningful souvenirs.

2. Local Art and Antiques

- **Handcrafted Jewelry**: For a more personal keepsake, consider Romanian handcrafted jewelry. Many local artisans create stunning pieces using traditional techniques and motifs. You'll find everything from intricately designed silver jewelry to colorful beaded pieces.

- **Folk Art and Paintings**: Bucharest's art galleries and craft shops offer a variety of folk art and paintings that depict Romanian landscapes, folklore, and historical scenes. These works make for memorable and culturally rich souvenirs.

3. Culinary Delights

    - **Romanian Wine and Spirits**: Romania has a burgeoning wine industry, and you can find excellent local wines and spirits, such as **țuica** (a traditional plum brandy). These make for a delightful gift for those who appreciate fine beverages.

    - **Traditional Sweets**: Bring home some traditional Romanian sweets, like **halva** (a sesame-based confection) or **cozonaci** (sweet bread). These treats will offer a taste of Romania long after you've left.

High-End Boutiques and Local Designers

For those who enjoy a touch of luxury and fashion, Bucharest is home to a range of high-end boutiques and local designers that cater to diverse tastes:

1. **High-End Boutiques**

- Cărturești Carusel: While primarily known as a bookstore, **Cărturești Carusel** also features a curated selection of luxury and designer goods, including fashion accessories and home décor items. Its stunning architecture and eclectic offerings make it a must-visit for style enthusiasts.

- Librarium: For a taste of Romanian luxury, **Librarium** offers high-end fashion items, accessories, and more. The boutique showcases both international brands and Romanian designers, providing a refined shopping experience.

2. **Local Designers**

- Rădăcini: This boutique is celebrated for its collection of contemporary Romanian fashion. **Rădăcini** features pieces from local designers who blend traditional Romanian elements with modern design, resulting in unique and stylish garments.

- **Andreea Tincu:** Known for her elegant and sophisticated designs, **Andreea Tincu** offers a range of clothing that combines high-quality fabrics with intricate craftsmanship. Her boutique is a great place to find a standout piece that reflects Romanian style.

- **Maria Lucia Hohan:** For glamorous and haute couture options, **Maria Lucia Hohan** is a top choice. Her boutique features luxurious evening wear and stylish outfits that are perfect for any special occasion.

Best Shopping Malls and Markets for Every Budget

Bucharest's shopping scene caters to all budgets, from high-end luxury to budget-friendly finds. Here's a guide to some of the city's best shopping malls and markets:

1. Shopping Malls

- **Băneasa Shopping City:** One of the largest and most popular shopping destinations in Bucharest, **Băneasa Shopping City** offers a wide range of stores, from luxury brands to high-street fashion. With over 300 shops, a food court, and entertainment options, it's a great place to spend a day shopping.

- AFI Cotroceni: Located in the Cotroceni district, **AFI Cotroceni** is another major shopping center that features a diverse range of retailers, including both international and local brands. The mall also has an extensive food court, a cinema, and various leisure activities.

- **Promenada Mall**: Situated in the northern part of the city, **Promenada Mall** offers a more upscale shopping experience. With a selection of high-end boutiques, gourmet dining options, and a stylish design, it's ideal for those seeking a more refined shopping environment.

2. Markets

- **Piața Unirii**: This bustling market is perfect for those looking for a lively shopping experience. **Piața Unirii** features a variety of vendors selling everything from fresh produce to clothing and accessories. It's a great place to experience local life and pick up some bargains.

- **Piața Obor**: As one of Bucharest's oldest markets, **Piața Obor** offers a vibrant atmosphere and a wide range of goods. From fresh fruits and vegetables to local cheeses and meats, this market is a treasure trove for foodies and bargain hunters alike.

- **Piața Amzei**: Known for its artisan products and local specialties, **Piața Amzei** is a great spot to explore Romanian crafts and culinary delights. The market's diverse offerings make it a fantastic place to find unique gifts and sample local flavors.

Bucharest's shopping landscape is as diverse as the city itself, offering everything from traditional crafts and high-end fashion to bustling markets and luxurious malls. Whether you're looking to bring home a piece of Romanian culture, indulge in luxury, or explore vibrant local markets, Bucharest provides a rich and varied shopping experience that caters to every taste and budget.

Outdoor Activities and Day Trips

Bucharest, often celebrated for its vibrant city life, also offers a wealth of outdoor activities and day trips that allow you to explore its natural beauty and historical treasures. Whether you're a fan of walking and biking tours, seeking peaceful green spaces, or planning a getaway from the city, there's something for everyone. Here's a comprehensive guide to enjoying Bucharest's outdoors and discovering the surrounding areas.

Walking and Biking Tours

1. Walking Tours

Exploring Bucharest on foot provides an intimate glimpse into the city's charm and historical layers. Walking tours allow you to soak in the architectural beauty, discover hidden gems, and experience the city's vibrant street life.

- **Historic Old Town (Lipscani District)**: Begin your walking adventure in the Old Town, where cobblestone streets and historic buildings create a picturesque backdrop. Highlights include the impressive **Palace of the Parliament**, charming **Stavropoleos Monastery**, and the bustling **Lipscani Street** filled with cafes, shops, and cultural landmarks. As you wander, take note of the eclectic mix of architectural styles, from neoclassical facades to ornate Art Nouveau details.

- **Calea Victoriei**: This historic avenue is one of Bucharest's most elegant streets. Stroll along **Calea Victoriei** to admire grandiose buildings such as the **Romanian Athenaeum**, the **National Museum of Art**, and the **Revolution Square**. The street's blend of old-world charm and modern vitality makes for a captivating walk.

2. Biking Tours

Biking is a fantastic way to cover more ground and enjoy Bucharest's green spaces and landmarks at a brisk pace. Several biking routes offer scenic views and access to key areas of interest.

- **Herăstrău Park Loop**: Start your biking journey at **Herăstrău Park**, the largest park in Bucharest. The park features a scenic lake, lush greenery, and well-maintained bike paths. Cycling around the lake offers panoramic views and the opportunity to stop at various attractions within the park, such as the **Village Museum** and numerous cafes.

- **Tineretului Park Circuit**: Another excellent biking route is **Tineretului Park**, a spacious green area with dedicated bike lanes. This park is ideal for a leisurely ride, with its expansive green lawns, picturesque lake, and various recreational facilities. It's a popular spot for both locals and visitors looking to enjoy a day outdoors.

Parks and Green Spaces for Relaxation

Bucharest's green spaces offer a welcome respite from the hustle and bustle of city life. These parks provide serene environments for relaxation, picnics, and leisurely strolls.

1. Herăstrău Park (King Michael I Park)

Herăstrău Park is Bucharest's largest and most beloved park, stretching over 187 hectares. It's a versatile space where you can enjoy a range of activities:

- Lake Herăstrău: The park's centerpiece is the lake, which offers opportunities for boating and peaceful lakeside walks. You can rent a pedal boat or simply sit by the water and enjoy the view.

- Village Museum: Located within the park, the **Village Museum** provides a fascinating glimpse into Romania's rural heritage with its collection of traditional houses and artifacts. It's a great place to explore while enjoying the park's natural beauty.

- Outdoor Cafes and Restaurants: Herăstrău Park also has a variety of outdoor cafes and restaurants where you can relax and savor a meal or a drink with a view of the lake.

2. Cismigiu Gardens

Cismigiu Gardens is a beautifully landscaped park situated in the heart of Bucharest. This historic park, dating back to the 19th century, offers a tranquil escape with its manicured gardens, serene lake, and charming pathways.

- **Cismigiu Lake:** The lake is a focal point of the park, where you can enjoy a leisurely boat ride or simply sit by the water's edge and watch the ducks. The surrounding greenery and flowerbeds create a picturesque setting.

- **Playgrounds and Sports Facilities:** The park also features playgrounds for children and sports facilities, making it a popular spot for families. The well-maintained walking paths are ideal for a relaxing stroll or a gentle jog.

3. Tineretului Park

Tineretului Park is another large and popular green space in Bucharest, known for its spacious layout and variety of recreational options.

- **The Lake:** The park's lake is a key feature, providing opportunities for boat rides and peaceful lakeside walks. The surrounding green areas are perfect for picnics and outdoor activities.

- **Sports and Recreation:** Tineretului Park includes sports facilities such as tennis courts and bike rental stations, making it an
- active and vibrant place for visitors.

Day Trips from Bucharest

Snagov Monastery, Mogoșoaia Palace, and More

For a change of pace and scenery, consider taking a day trip from Bucharest to explore nearby historical and natural attractions. These destinations offer a glimpse into Romania's rich cultural heritage and scenic beauty.

1. Snagov Monastery

Located about 40 kilometers north of Bucharest, **Snagov Monastery** is situated on an island in Lake Snagov. This historic monastery is renowned for its picturesque setting and its association with Vlad the Impaler, the figure who inspired the Dracula legend.

- **Monastic Architecture**: The monastery's architecture is a blend of Byzantine and Romanian styles, with beautiful frescoes and a serene atmosphere. It's a peaceful place to explore and reflect.

- **Scenic Lake Views**: The journey to Snagov Monastery involves a short boat ride across the lake, offering scenic views and a tranquil experience away from the city.

2. Mogoșoaia Palace

Approximately 15 kilometers northwest of Bucharest, **Mogoșoaia Palace** is a stunning example of Romanian Renaissance architecture. Built in the early 17th century, the palace is surrounded by beautiful gardens and a serene park.

- **Architectural Beauty**: The palace's architecture features intricate stonework and ornate interiors. The spacious gardens and parkland add to the palace's charm, providing a lovely setting for a leisurely stroll.

- **Cultural Events**: The palace often hosts cultural events, exhibitions, and performances, making it a vibrant place to visit. Check the schedule for any special events during your visit.

3. Peles Castle

A bit further afield, about 120 kilometers from Bucharest, **Peles Castle** is a fairy-tale castle nestled in the Carpathian Mountains. Located in Sinaia, this neo-Renaissance castle is renowned for its opulent interiors and stunning mountain views.

- **Castle Tour**: Explore the richly decorated rooms, including the Great Hall and the Royal Apartments. The castle's intricate woodwork and luxurious furnishings reflect the grandeur of Romania's royal history.

- **Surrounding Nature**: The castle is set amidst lush forests and mountain scenery, making it a picturesque spot for hiking and exploring the natural beauty of the region.

Bucharest offers a diverse range of outdoor activities and day trips, from exploring the city's green spaces and cycling paths to venturing out to nearby historical and natural landmarks. Whether you're seeking relaxation or adventure, these experiences will help you make the most of your time in and around Romania's vibrant capital.

Accommodation

Finding the right place to stay can make or break your trip, and Bucharest offers a wide range of accommodation options to suit every type of traveler. From opulent luxury hotels and charming boutique stays to budget-friendly hostels and cozy Airbnbs, there's something for everyone. Here's an in-depth look at Bucharest's accommodation scene, including tips on where to stay, depending on your preferences and needs.

Luxury Hotels and Boutique Stays

For those seeking a touch of elegance and top-notch amenities, Bucharest's luxury hotels and boutique accommodations provide a sophisticated and comfortable stay.

1. Luxury Hotels

- **Athenee Palace Hilton Bucharest**: Located in the heart of the city, this iconic hotel combines historic charm with modern luxury. The Athenee Palace Hilton is renowned for its stunning architecture, elegant rooms, and impeccable service. Guests can enjoy fine dining at the hotel's restaurant, relax in the stylish bar, or take advantage of the spa and fitness facilities. Its central location makes it an ideal choice for exploring Bucharest's top attractions.

- **JW Marriott Bucharest Grand Hotel**: This five-star hotel is known for its grandeur and extensive amenities. The JW Marriott offers spacious rooms, a luxurious spa, a variety of dining options, and a casino. The hotel's location near the Palace of the Parliament provides easy access to major landmarks and a touch of opulence.

- **Radisson Blu Hotel Bucharest**: A blend of contemporary style and classic comfort, the Radisson Blu features a range of well-appointed rooms, an indoor pool, a fitness center, and multiple dining options. Its central location makes it convenient for both business and leisure travelers.

2. Boutique Stays

- **Zava Boutique Hotel**: For a more personalized experience, Zava Boutique Hotel offers stylish and unique accommodations in a charming setting. The hotel's design blends modern aesthetics with classic touches, creating a cozy and inviting atmosphere. Located in a quieter part of the city, it provides a relaxing retreat with easy access to local attractions.

- **The Mansion Boutique Hotel**: This boutique hotel combines historical elegance with contemporary comfort. Housed in a beautifully restored mansion, The Mansion offers individually decorated rooms, a gourmet restaurant, and a tranquil garden. It's a perfect choice for travelers looking for a distinctive and intimate lodging experience.

Budget Hotels, Hostels, and Airbnbs

Travelers on a tighter budget can still enjoy a comfortable stay in Bucharest, thanks to a range of affordable hotels, hostels, and vacation rentals.

1. Budget Hotels

- **Ibis Bucharest Gara de Nord**: A reliable and budget-friendly option, Ibis offers comfortable rooms with modern amenities. Its proximity to the train station makes it a convenient choice for travelers arriving by train. The hotel provides a straightforward and affordable stay without sacrificing quality.

- **Hotel Cismigiu:** Situated near Cismigiu Gardens, this hotel offers a great balance of comfort and value. Guests can enjoy cozy rooms, friendly service, and easy access to local attractions and green spaces.

2. Hostels

- **Podstel Bucharest:** Known for its vibrant atmosphere and welcoming staff, Podstel offers a range of dormitory-style and private rooms. The hostel's communal spaces are perfect for meeting fellow travelers, and its central location provides easy access to the city's sights and nightlife.

- **The Cozyness Hostel:** This hostel is celebrated for its cleanliness, comfort, and friendly environment. With a variety of room options, including both dorms and private rooms, The Cozyness Hostel offers an affordable and pleasant stay in a convenient location.

3. Airbnbs

- **Charming Studio in Old Town:** For a more home-like experience, consider renting a charming studio in Bucharest's Old

Town. These rentals often feature stylish decor, modern amenities, and a prime location, allowing you to immerse yourself in the city's vibrant atmosphere.

- **Modern Apartment Near Herăstrău Park:** If you prefer a bit more space, a modern apartment near Herăstrău Park provides a comfortable and private stay. With easy access to the park's green spaces and a range of local dining options, it's an excellent choice for a longer stay or a family trip.

Neighborhood Guide

Where to Stay for First-Time Visitors

Choosing the right neighborhood can greatly enhance your experience in Bucharest. Here's a guide to the best areas for first-time visitors, based on their preferences and interests:

1. Old Town (Lipscani District)

Old Town is Bucharest's historic and cultural heart, ideal for those who want to be in the midst of the city's vibrant nightlife, dining, and cultural attractions. Staying here places you within walking distance of key landmarks like the Palace of the Parliament, Stavropoleos Monastery, and numerous cafes and bars. The area's cobblestone streets and historic architecture add to its charm, making it a popular choice for first-time visitors.

2. Piata Unirii

Piata Unirii is a central and convenient location, offering easy access to major transportation links and shopping areas. The large square and surrounding area are home to several hotels, restaurants, and shopping centers. Staying here provides a practical base with excellent connectivity to other parts of the city, including a direct route to Bucharest's major attractions.

3. Herăstrău

Herăstrău is perfect for travelers seeking a blend of urban and natural experiences. Located near Herăstrău Park, this area offers a tranquil setting with easy access to green spaces, walking trails, and cultural institutions like the Village Museum. It's an excellent choice for those who enjoy outdoor activities and a more relaxed pace, while still being close to the city center.

4. Cotroceni

Cotroceni is a charming residential neighborhood known for its historical architecture and proximity to the Cotroceni Palace. This area provides a more peaceful environment while still being within reach of Bucharest's main attractions. It's ideal for visitors who prefer a quieter stay with a touch of local flavor.

Bucharest offers a diverse range of accommodation options to suit every type of traveler. From luxurious hotels and boutique stays to budget-friendly hostels and cozy Airbnbs, there's something to meet every preference and budget. By choosing the right place to stay and the best neighborhood for your interests, you can ensure a memorable and enjoyable visit to Romania's vibrant capital.

Seasonal Events and Festivals

Bucharest's vibrant cultural scene comes alive throughout the year with a diverse array of festivals and seasonal events that highlight the city's rich artistic heritage and local traditions. Whether you're a music enthusiast, an art lover, or simply looking to immerse yourself in Romanian culture, there's a festival or event that's sure to captivate you. Here's an extensive look at the seasonal events and festivals in Bucharest, including music and arts festivals, holiday celebrations, and the best times to visit for cultural experiences.

Bucharest Music and Arts Festivals

1. George Enescu Festival

One of the most prestigious music festivals in Romania, the **George Enescu Festival** is a celebration of classical music held biennially in Bucharest. Named after the renowned Romanian composer George Enescu, this festival attracts top international orchestras, soloists, and conductors.

- **Program Highlights:** The festival features a diverse program, including symphonic concerts, chamber music, and opera performances. Expect to hear works by Enescu himself, as well as masterpieces from composers like Beethoven, Brahms, and Tchaikovsky.

- **Venue:** Performances take place at various venues across Bucharest, including the **Romanian Athenaeum** and the **National Theatre Bucharest**. The festival's high caliber and prestigious reputation make it a must-attend for classical music aficionados.

2. Bucharest International Dance Film Festival

The **Bucharest International Dance Film Festival** is an exciting event that combines dance and film, showcasing innovative works from around the world. This festival celebrates the intersection of dance and cinema, offering a unique platform for artists to present their creative visions.

- **Program Highlights**: The festival features a range of dance films, including short films, documentaries, and experimental works. Workshops and masterclasses with industry professionals provide additional opportunities for learning and engagement.

- **Venue:** Screenings and events are held at various locations, including cultural centers and cinemas across the city. The festival's eclectic program ensures a dynamic and inspiring experience for attendees.

3. Bucharest Jazz Festival

Jazz enthusiasts will find plenty to enjoy at the **Bucharest Jazz Festival**, which highlights both local and international jazz talent. This annual event celebrates the diverse styles and improvisational nature of jazz music.

- **Program Highlights**: Expect performances from renowned jazz musicians, including both established artists and emerging talents. The festival often features a mix of solo performances, ensembles, and jam sessions.

- **Venue**: The festival takes place at various venues, including jazz clubs and open-air spaces, creating an intimate and engaging atmosphere for music lovers.

Holiday Celebrations and Traditions

1. Christmas Markets and Festivities

Bucharest transforms into a winter wonderland during the Christmas season, with festive markets and celebrations that bring holiday cheer to the city.

- **Christmas Market at University Square**: One of the main attractions is the Christmas Market at **University Square**, where visitors can browse a variety of stalls selling handcrafted gifts, holiday decorations, and traditional Romanian foods. The market is also adorned with twinkling lights and festive decorations, creating a magical atmosphere.

- **Holiday Concerts and Events**: Throughout December, Bucharest hosts a series of holiday concerts and events, including performances of traditional Christmas carols and seasonal music at venues like the **Romanian Athenaeum** and **National Theatre Bucharest**.

2. Romanian Easter Traditions

Easter in Romania is marked by a range of traditional celebrations and customs, reflecting the country's rich cultural heritage.

- **Pascal Services and Celebrations**: Attend a traditional Easter service at one of Bucharest's historic churches, such as the **Stavropoleos Monastery**. The service is often accompanied by festive music and a sense of communal celebration.

- **Easter Markets and Feasts**: Explore local markets to find traditional Easter foods, including painted eggs, lamb dishes, and sweet pastries. Bucharest's restaurants and cafes also offer special Easter menus featuring these traditional delicacies.

3. Romanian National Day

Celebrated on December 1st, **Romanian National Day** commemorates the unification of the Romanian principalities in 1918. The day is marked by patriotic events and public celebrations.

- **Parades and Ceremonies**: Experience the festive atmosphere of parades and military ceremonies held across the city. Public squares, such as **Revolution Square**, host performances, speeches, and displays of national pride.

- **Cultural Events**: Various cultural events, including music performances and folk dance shows, take place throughout the city, offering a glimpse into Romania's national identity and traditions.

Best Times to Visit for Cultural Experiences

1. Spring (April to June)

Spring is an excellent time to visit Bucharest for cultural experiences. The weather is mild and pleasant, making it ideal for exploring the city's outdoor attractions and attending festivals.

- **Events**: Enjoy the early festivals of the season, such as the **Bucharest International Dance Film Festival** and various local arts events. The blooming gardens and parks add to the city's charm during this time.

2. Summer (July to August)

Summer brings a lively atmosphere to Bucharest, with numerous outdoor events and festivals taking place. The warm weather and extended daylight hours make it a great time to enjoy the city's cultural offerings.

- **Events**: Summer is the season for major music festivals like the **George Enescu Festival**, as well as outdoor concerts and cultural fairs. The city's vibrant nightlife and outdoor dining options also come to life.

3. Autumn (September to November)

Autumn is another prime time for cultural experiences in Bucharest. The cooler temperatures and colorful fall foliage provide a beautiful backdrop for exploring the city's historic sites and attending festivals.

- Events: The **George Enescu Festival** continues into early autumn, offering world-class music performances. The season also features various local arts and cultural events, as well as the start of the holiday preparations.

4. Winter (December to February)

Winter in Bucharest is magical, with festive holiday celebrations and a cozy atmosphere that invites exploration of the city's cultural and historical sites.

- Events: Experience the charm of Bucharest's Christmas markets, holiday concerts, and traditional Easter celebrations. The city's festive decorations and seasonal events create a warm and inviting environment, even in the colder months.

Bucharest's seasonal events and festivals offer a rich tapestry of cultural experiences that reflect the city's dynamic spirit and deep-rooted traditions. Whether you're visiting for a music festival, a holiday celebration, or simply to enjoy the vibrant cultural scene, Bucharest has something to offer year-round.

Practical Travel Tips

Traveling to Bucharest can be an exciting adventure, and being well-prepared will help ensure a smooth and enjoyable experience. Here's an extensive guide to practical travel tips, covering everything from currency and safety to health and staying connected.

Currency, ATMs, and Credit Cards

1. **Currency**

Bucharest's official currency is the Romanian Leu (RON). It's essential to have some local currency on hand for smaller transactions, such as street food or local markets, where card payments might not always be accepted.

- **Currency Exchange:** You can exchange your money at banks, exchange offices, or even at some hotels. It's advisable to use official exchange offices or banks to avoid unfavorable rates or potential scams. Be sure to check the exchange rate beforehand to ensure you're getting a fair deal.

- **Cash vs. Card:** While many establishments in Bucharest accept credit and debit cards, cash is still commonly used. Having a small amount of cash will be helpful for places that don't accept cards or for small purchases.

2. ATMs

ATMs are widely available throughout Bucharest, including at airports, major train stations, and in various neighborhoods.

- **Using ATMs:** Most ATMs accept international cards, including Visa and MasterCard. Be cautious of fees and exchange rates that might apply when withdrawing cash. It's a good idea to use ATMs located in well-lit, secure areas, such as those in bank branches or shopping centers.

- **ATM Safety**: When using ATMs, ensure you're in a secure location, and be mindful of your surroundings. Cover your PIN while entering it and avoid withdrawing large sums of money at once.

3. Credit Cards

Credit cards are widely accepted in Bucharest, especially in hotels, restaurants, and larger stores.

- **Card Usage**: Major credit cards like Visa and MasterCard are commonly accepted. American Express may not be as widely accepted, so it's wise to carry a backup card.

- **Notify Your Bank**: Before traveling, inform your bank or credit card company of your trip to avoid any issues with your cards being flagged for suspicious activity. This also helps ensure you have access to your funds without interruption.

Safety Tips for Tourists

Bucharest is generally a safe city for tourists, but it's always wise to take some basic precautions to ensure a trouble-free visit.

1. General Safety

- **Stay Vigilant**: As with any major city, be aware of your surroundings and keep an eye on your belongings, especially in crowded areas like public transportation and tourist hotspots.

- **Avoid Risky Areas**: While Bucharest is safe, there are areas that are best avoided at night. Stick to well-lit and populated areas, particularly if you're exploring after dark.

2. Scams and Petty Crime

- **Common Scams**: Be cautious of common tourist scams, such as overcharging or being approached by individuals asking for money or offering unsolicited help. If something feels off, trust your instincts and walk away.

- **Pickpocketing**: Pickpocketing can occur in crowded areas and on public transport. Use anti-theft bags and keep your valuables secure. Consider using a money belt or a secure pouch for important items like passports and cash.

3. **Emergency Services**

- **Emergency Numbers**: In case of emergency, dial 112 for police, fire, or medical assistance. This is the European Union's emergency number and will connect you to the appropriate services.

- **Local Contacts**: It's useful to have the contact information for your country's embassy or consulate in Romania. They can provide assistance in case of legal or emergency issues.

Health and Emergency Information

1. Health Precautions

- **Vaccinations**: Check with your healthcare provider for any recommended vaccinations before traveling to Romania. Standard travel vaccines are usually sufficient, but it's always best to get personalized advice based on your health and travel history.

- **Travel Insurance**: Consider purchasing travel insurance that covers medical emergencies, trip cancellations, and lost or stolen belongings. This provides peace of mind and ensures you're covered in case of unexpected events.

2. Medical Care

- **Healthcare Facilities**: Bucharest has a range of healthcare facilities, from public hospitals to private clinics. In case of medical issues, private clinics often offer quicker service and English-speaking staff.

- **Pharmacies**: Pharmacies are widespread and can provide over-the-counter medications as well as prescriptions. They are often labeled "Farmacie" and can be found throughout the city.

3. Emergency Contacts

- **Hospitals and Clinics**: If you need medical assistance, hospitals such as the **Floreasca Emergency Hospital** or **Bucharest Hospital** offer emergency care. Private clinics like **Medicover** and **Regina Maria** also provide high-quality services.

- **Medical Assistance**: If you need immediate medical help, call 112 for an ambulance. Ensure you have the address and details of your location ready to provide to the operator.

Internet, SIM Cards, and Staying Connected

1. Internet Access

- **Wi-Fi**: Bucharest offers widespread Wi-Fi access in cafes, restaurants, hotels, and public areas. Many establishments provide free Wi-Fi for customers, so you can stay connected while enjoying a meal or coffee.

- **Cafes and Libraries**: Public places such as cafes and libraries are excellent spots for accessing the internet. They often offer free Wi-Fi and provide a comfortable setting for checking emails or planning your day.

2. SIM Cards and Mobile Data

- **Purchasing SIM Cards**: For more extensive internet access, consider purchasing a local SIM card. SIM cards are available at airports, mobile network stores, and convenience stores. Major providers include **Orange**, **Vodafone**, and **Digi Mobil**.

- **Prepaid Plans**: Look for prepaid plans that offer data, local calls, and text messaging. These plans are often more cost-effective than roaming charges and provide flexible options based on your needs.

3. Staying Connected

- Roaming Services: If you prefer to use your existing mobile plan, check with your provider about international roaming options. Be aware of potential high charges and consider activating a roaming plan that suits your travel needs.

- Local SIM Cards: For extended stays or frequent travelers, getting a local SIM card offers a more economical solution for staying connected. Ensure your phone is unlocked and compatible with Romanian networks.

Navigating Bucharest with these practical travel tips will help you make the most of your visit while ensuring a smooth and enjoyable experience. From handling currency and staying safe to accessing healthcare and staying connected, being prepared will allow you to focus on exploring and enjoying the vibrant culture and history of Romania's capital.

Sample Itineraries

Whether you're in Bucharest for a brief visit or planning an extended stay, having a well-crafted itinerary can help you make the most of your time in this vibrant city. Here are some sample itineraries tailored to different lengths of stay, designed to provide a comprehensive and enjoyable experience.

3 Days in Bucharest

Day 1: Historic Core and Iconic Landmarks

- **Morning:**
    - Start your day at the **Palace of the Parliament**, an awe-inspiring example of Communist-era architecture. Take a guided tour to explore its opulent halls and learn about its controversial history.

- o Walk over to **Old Town (Lipscani)**, where you can wander through narrow cobblestone streets, admire historical buildings, and visit landmarks like the **Stavropoleos Monastery**.
- **Afternoon:**
  - o Enjoy a leisurely lunch at one of the charming cafes in Old Town. Try traditional Romanian dishes such as **sarmale** (cabbage rolls) or **mici** (grilled sausages).
  - o Visit the **National Museum of Romanian History** to delve into the country's rich past. The museum's exhibits offer insights into Romanian culture, from ancient times to the modern era.
- **Evening:**
  - o Head to **Cismigiu Gardens** for a relaxing evening stroll. This beautiful park is a perfect spot to unwind and enjoy the tranquil atmosphere.

- Have dinner at a local restaurant in Old Town and experience Bucharest's vibrant nightlife with a visit to a nearby bar or pub.

Day 2: Cultural Immersion and Green Spaces

- Morning:
    - Begin with a visit to the **Romanian Athenaeum**, a stunning concert hall known for its classical music performances. Take a guided tour if available to appreciate its architectural beauty and historical significance.
    - Explore **Herăstrău Park** (now known as **King Michael I Park**), where you can enjoy a boat ride on the lake or simply relax by the water.
- Afternoon:
    - Head to the **Village Museum** to gain insight into Romanian rural life. This open-air museum showcases traditional Romanian houses, crafts, and agricultural tools.

- Grab lunch at a nearby restaurant, savoring local specialties or international cuisine.
- **Evening:**
  - Enjoy an evening of live music at one of Bucharest's popular venues. Whether it's jazz, rock, or classical, the city's music scene offers a variety of options.
  - Dine at a restaurant with a view, such as a rooftop bar, and soak in the city's evening ambiance.

Day 3: Artistic Flair and Final Explorations

- **Morning:**
  - Visit the **National Museum of Art of Romania**, which houses an extensive collection of Romanian medieval and modern art. This museum provides a deep dive into the country's artistic heritage.
  - Take a walk through **University Square** and see landmarks like the **National Theatre Bucharest**.

- **Afternoon:**
    - Enjoy a late lunch in one of the city's trendy neighborhoods, such as **Piata Victoriei** or **Unirii Square**.
    - Spend your afternoon shopping for souvenirs or exploring any last-minute sights you've missed.
- **Evening:**
    - Have a farewell dinner at a restaurant of your choice, perhaps one you've discovered earlier in your stay.
    - If time allows, enjoy one last evening walk through Bucharest's illuminated streets or a final visit to a favorite spot.

5-Day Cultural and Historical Exploration

Day 1: Introduction to Bucharest

- Follow the itinerary for Day 1 from the 3-day plan, covering major landmarks and Old Town.

Day 2: In-Depth Historical Insights

- **Morning:**
    - Visit the **Museum of the Romanian Peasant** to learn about traditional Romanian folk culture and art.
    - Explore the **Revolution Square** and the **National Museum of Contemporary Art**, housed in the Palace of the Parliament.

- **Afternoon:**
    - Enjoy lunch at a local eatery and then visit the **Arch of Triumph** and **King Michael I Park** for more historical context and relaxation.

- **Evening:**
    - Dine at a traditional Romanian restaurant and explore more of Bucharest's nightlife.

Day 3: Artistic and Architectural Wonders

- Morning:

    - Start with a visit to the **Romanian Athenaeum** and then head to the **Bucharest Botanical Garden** for a peaceful morning among nature.

    - Explore **Cotroceni Palace**, the official residence of the Romanian president, offering insights into modern Romanian politics and history.

- Afternoon:

    - Have lunch at a nearby restaurant and visit the **National Museum of Art of Romania** to explore its rich collections.

- Evening:

    - Experience a theater performance or a concert at one of Bucharest's historic venues.

Day 4: Day Trip to Snagov

- **Morning and Afternoon:**
    - Take a day trip to **Snagov Monastery**, located on an island in Snagov Lake. This historical site is known for its association with Vlad the Impaler.
    - Enjoy a lakeside lunch and explore the surrounding natural beauty.

- **Evening:**
    - Return to Bucharest and enjoy a relaxed evening with dinner at a local restaurant.

Day 5: Modern Bucharest and Shopping

- **Morning:**
    - Visit the **Bucharest Mall** or **Baneasa Shopping City** for some shopping and modern city experiences.
    - Explore the **Palace of the Parliament** if you haven't yet, or take a final stroll through **Old Town**.

- Afternoon:
    - Have lunch at a trendy cafe or bistro and enjoy your last afternoon in the city.
- Evening:
    - Celebrate your final night with a special dinner or a visit to a local bar with live music.

One Week in Bucharest

In-Depth Discovery of the City

Day 1-3: Follow the 3-Day Itinerary

Day 4: Explore Surroundings and Day Trips

- Morning:
    - Take a day trip to **Mogosoaia Palace**, a beautiful example of Brancovenesc architecture, set in a picturesque park.

- **Afternoon:**
    - Enjoy lunch at a local restaurant and explore the palace grounds.
    - Return to Bucharest and have a relaxed evening.

Day 5: Discover Local Neighborhoods

- **Morning:**
    - Explore neighborhoods like **Piata Romana** and **Dorobanti**, known for their unique architecture, shops, and local life.
- **Afternoon:**
    - Visit the **National Museum of the Romanian Literature** and enjoy lunch at a nearby restaurant.
- **Evening:**
    - Experience Bucharest's dining scene at a fine restaurant and take an evening stroll through **Revolution Square**.

Day 6: Cultural and Historical Immersion

- Morning:
    - Visit the **National Museum of History** and **Museum of the Romanian Revolution** to deepen your understanding of Romania's past.
- Afternoon:
    - Have lunch at a traditional restaurant and then visit the **Bucharest City Museum**.
- Evening:
    - Enjoy a cultural performance or a relaxed evening exploring local cafes.

Day 7: Leisure and Relaxation

- Morning:
    - Spend your final day leisurely exploring any remaining sites or revisiting your favorite spots.
    - Relax at **Cismigiu Gardens** or **Herăstrău Park**.

- **Afternoon:**
    - Do some last-minute shopping or explore any areas you may have missed.
- **Evening:**
    - Celebrate your last night in Bucharest with a special dinner and a final evening walk through the illuminated city streets.

Weekend Getaways

Exploring Bucharest and Beyond

Day 1: Bucharest Highlights

- **Morning:**
    - Start your weekend with a visit to the **Palace of the Parliament** and **Old Town**.
    - Enjoy lunch at a local restaurant in Old Town.

- Afternoon:
    - Explore **Cismigiu Gardens** and visit the **National Museum of Romanian History**.
- Evening:
    - Experience Bucharest's nightlife with dinner and drinks in Old Town.

Day 2: Day Trip to Peles Castle

- Morning and Afternoon:
    - Take a day trip to **Peles Castle** in Sinaia, a stunning Neo-Renaissance castle nestled in the Carpathian Mountains.
    - Enjoy a guided tour of the castle and lunch at a local restaurant in Sinaia.
- Evening:
    - Return to Bucharest and have a relaxed evening.

Bucharest Travel Guide 2025

Day 3: Bucharest's Local Experiences

- **Morning:**
  - Explore **Piata Victoriei** and visit the **Romanian Athenaeum** if you haven't yet.
  - Enjoy brunch at a local cafe.
- **Afternoon:**
  - Visit a local market or do some shopping for souvenirs.
  - Take a leisurely stroll through a neighborhood like **Dorobanti**.
- **Evening:**
  - Have a farewell dinner at a restaurant of your choice and enjoy a final evening in Bucharest.

These sample itineraries are designed to help you experience the best of Bucharest, whether you're staying for a few days or a week. Each itinerary provides a mix of cultural, historical, and leisure activities, ensuring a well-rounded visit to Romania's vibrant capital.

Conclusion

Embracing the Charm of Bucharest

As your journey through Bucharest draws to a close, take a moment to reflect on the rich tapestry of experiences that this vibrant city has woven into your travel story. Bucharest, with its captivating blend of historical grandeur and modern vibrancy, offers more than just a destination—it provides a mosaic of memories that linger long after you've departed.

In just a few days, you've walked the storied streets of Old Town, marveled at the colossal Palace of the Parliament, and been enchanted by the serene beauty of Cismigiu Gardens. You've dined on delicious local dishes, discovered hidden gems like the Stavropoleos Monastery, and immersed yourself in Romania's complex and fascinating history. From the striking contrasts of neoclassical and brutalist architecture to the lively rhythms of its nightlife, Bucharest reveals itself as a city of contrasts and surprises.

Bucharest's charm lies in its ability to blend the old with the new, the traditional with the modern. The grandiose remnants of its communist past coexist with a dynamic cultural scene and a thriving artistic community. Whether you were captivated by the stories of revolution, the echoes of classical music, or the bustling energy of its markets, Bucharest offers something for every traveler.

But beyond the sites and activities, it's the warmth of the people and the spirit of the city that truly make Bucharest memorable. Each interaction, whether with a local shopkeeper, a fellow traveler, or a friendly guide, adds a personal touch to your experience. The city's genuine hospitality and the rhythm of everyday life contribute to a sense of belonging that transforms a visit into something more profound.

As you prepare to leave, remember that Bucharest is not just a destination but a collection of moments and experiences that will stay with you. The city's rich history, vibrant culture, and dynamic energy create a narrative that invites you to return. Each visit offers a new chapter, a fresh perspective on a city that is constantly evolving while remaining deeply rooted in its past.

So, as you say goodbye to Bucharest, carry with you the stories of its past and the promise of its future. Let the memories of its grand architecture, lively streets, and welcoming people be a testament to your journey. And know that the essence of Bucharest—its spirit, its stories, and its soul—will always be with you, ready to inspire your next adventure.

In the end, Bucharest isn't just a place on a map; it's a living, breathing experience that invites you to explore, to engage, and to be inspired. Safe travels and may your future adventures be as rich and rewarding as the time you've spent in this remarkable city.

Printed in Great Britain
by Amazon